MYTHOLOGY OF NORTHERN EUROPE

WILLIAM DARLINGTON

FV Editions

CONTENTS

1. Odin; his conquests; his arrival in the North, and the changes he there made. — 1
2. General Idea of the Ancient Religion of Northern Europe. — 10
3. Of the religion of Northern Europe, since Odin. — 14
4. Tenets of the Celts in reference to the future state, and to the last destinies of this world. — 34
5. Progress of the Religion of the People of the North. — 44
6. Researches into the ancient religion of the primitive inhabitants of Great Britain. — 55
7. Religious tenets of the primitive inhabitants of Great Britain. — 64
8. Of the Druids. — 70
9. Of the different classes of Priests; their manner of living; their dress and functions. — 75
10. Doctrine of the Druids; their Superstitions; ceremony of the Oak-misletoe. — 80

11. Principal Maxims of the Druids. 86
12. Of the Druidesses. 89

ODIN; HIS CONQUESTS; HIS ARRIVAL IN THE NORTH, AND THE CHANGES HE THERE MADE.

A celebrated tradition, confirmed by all the poesies of Northern Europe, by the annals of the people, by their institutions, and by their ancient usages, (some of which still exist,) informs us that an extraordinary personage, named Odin, anciently reigned there; that he performed great changes in government, in manners, customs, and religion; that he exercised great authority; and that he received even divine honours. These facts cannot be contested; but the origin of this wonderful man, the country which gave him birth, the time in which he flourished, and various other circumstances of his life, are enveloped in a cloud of obscurity, impenetrable to the acute eye of research. All the testimonies which deserve any sort of confidence are comprised in a work of

Snorron, an ancient historian of Norway, together with the commentaries which Torfacus has added to his account.

The Roman republic was at its acme of power, and found nothing in the known parts of the world which did not acknowledge her laws, when an event occurred that raised her up enemies even in the heart of the Scythian forests, and on the banks of the Tanais. Mithridates flying thither attracted Pompey into the deserts. This king of Pontus there sought an asylum, and, also, means of revenge. Accordingly, he attempted to arm against the ambition of Rome, all the barbarian nations whose liberties she threatened. His first efforts appeared to be successful; but these people proved faithless to him — ill-armed, undisciplined soldiers — who were soon compelled to yield to the genius of Pompey. Odin, it is said, was among this number. Obliged to fly from the pursuit of the Romans, he sought in countries unknown to his enemies, that liberty which he found not in his own. His real name was *Frige*, son of *Fridulphe*. He assumed that of Odin, the supreme god of the Scythians, either that he might be considered a man inspired by the gods, or because he was the first priest or the chief of the worship which was paid to the god Odin. It is known that several nations gave their pontiffs the name of the god whom they served. Frige, filled with his ambitious projects, did not fail to usurp a name which was calculated to secure to him the respect of the people whom he wished to bring into subjection.

Odin ruled, it is said, the *Ases*, a Scythian people, whose country was situated between the Black and the Caspian seas. Their principal city was *Asgard*. The worship paid to the supreme god, was celebrated in all neighbouring countries; and it was Odin who performed the functions of this worship, as a chief, aided by twelve other pontiffs, a sort of druids, who also administered justice (Drotars.) Odin, having united under his standard the flower of the neighbouring countries, marched towards the Northern and Western boundaries of Europe, subduing all who opposed his progress, and leaving some of his sons to rule over them. Thus *Suavlami* had Russia; *Baldeg*, Western Saxony or Westphalia; *Segdeg*, Eastern Saxony; and *Sigge*, Franconia. Most of the sovereign families of the North are descended from these self-same princes. Thus, *Horsa* and *Hengist*, chiefs of those Saxons who subdued Britain in the fifth century, counted Odin or Woden in the number of their ancestors. The same was true of other Anglo-Saxon princes. The name of Odin, therefore, ultimately came to signify the supreme god of the Scythians and Celts. It is also known that the heroes of all these nations, pretended to be descended from their gods, and especially from the god of war. The historians of those times, (that is to say, the poets,) granted the same honour to those whose praises they sung; and thus multiplied the descendants of Odin, or of the supreme god.

After having forced many nations to adopt the worship of his country, Odin took the route to Scandinavia, by *Chersonesus Cimbrica*. These provinces did not resist him; and, soon after, he passed into *Fionia*, which immediately became his conquest. In this pleasant island, it is said; he made a long stay, and built the city of *Odensus*, which still perpetuates in its name, the remembrance of its founder. Thence he extended his arms over the whole North. In Denmark, he caused his son *Sciold* to be acknowledged king, a title which no ruler of that country had yet borne, (according to the annals of Iceland,) and which passed to his descendants, called from his name *Scioldungians*.

Odin more pleased with giving crowns to his sons than with reigning himself, next repaired to Sweden, where reigned a prince named *Gylphe*, who, regarding the author of a new worship, renowned and consecrated by such brilliant conquests, as an extraordinary being, loaded him with great honours, and adored him even as a divinity. This reception, favoured by the ignorance of the people, soon acquired him in Sweden the same authority as in Denmark. The Swedes came in crowds to pay him homage, and unanimously yielded the title and power of king to his son *Yngue*, which descended to his remoter posterity. Hence, the *Ynglinglians*, a name which has long served to designate the first kings of Sweden, Gylphe died, or was forgotten. Odin governed with absolute dominion. He made new laws introduced the usages of his country, established at Sigutna (a city situated in the same province with Stockholm, but now extinct,) a supreme council or tribunal, composed of twelve lords or druids. They were appointed to watch over the public safety, to administer justice to the people, to preside over the new worship, and faithfully to preserve the deposit of the religious and magic sciences of this prince.

So many conquests had not yet satisfied his ambition. The desire of spreading his religion, his glory, and authority, made him undertake the subjugation of Norway. His good fortune and great abilities attended him thither. This kingdom soon obeyed a son of Odin, named *Sæmungue*, who did not fail of being made the author of the family, whose different branches afterwards reigned long in the same country.

After these glorious expeditions, Odin retired into Sweden, where, feeling his end draw near, he would not await, through the series of a disease, that death which he had so many times braved in battle. Having assembled his friends and his companions, he inflicted upon himself, with the point of a lance, nine wounds, in the form of a circle, and divers other cut-paper works in his skin with his sword. Whilst dying, he declared that he was going into Scythia, to take his place with the other gods at an eternal banquet, where he would receive, with great honours, those who, after having exposed themselves courageously in battle, should die with arms in their hands. As soon as he had breathed his last, his body was carried to Sigutna, where, conformably to the usage which he had brought into the North, it was burnt with great pomp and magnificence.

Such was the end of this man, no less extraordinary in his death than in his life. Some learned men have supposed that the desire of revenging himself upon the Romans was the principle of all his actions. Driven by those enemies of all liberty, from his native country, his resentment was truly Scythian, as every Scythian considered it a sacred duty to avenge injuries, and especially those of his relatives and country. The grand object of Odin, therefore, in travelling over remote countries, and so ardently establishing his doctrines, was to raise up enemies against an odious and formidable power. This old grudge long fermented secretly in the minds of the Northern Nations; and when the signal was given, they rushed, with one accord, upon that ambitious empire, and finally avenged themselves, as well as the injuries done to their founder and to all those whom she had stripped and trampled under her feet, by overwhelming and crushing her gigantic power.

I cannot resolve, says Mr. Mallet, to make objections against so ingenious a narrative as this account of Odin, although it gives too much importance to the history of the North, by putting into it too much interest, too much poesy, so to speak, so that I can scarcely consent to yield to the various proofs which have been adduced in its favour. It is, doubtless, more rational to see in Odin only the founder of a new worship, previously unknown to the Scandinavians. It is also probable that he, his father, or the author of this religion, whoever he was, came from Scythia, or the confines of Persia; and still more so, that the name of the god whose prophet and priest he became, was, in succeeding ages, transferred to him, and the attributes of the deity confounded with the history of the priest. The accounts of Odin preserved by the Icelanders, confirm these conjectures.

One of the artifices which he employed with the greatest success, in order to secure to himself the confidence and respect of the people was to consult, in difficult affairs, the head of a certain Mimer, who, during his life, had a great reputation for wisdom. This man having had his head cut off, Odin embalmed it, and knew how to persuade the Scandinavians that he had given him speech by his enchantments. He always carried it with him, and made it pronounce the oracles of which he stood in need. This artifice reminds us of the pigeon which carried to Mahomet the orders of Heaven, and shows the superstition of those who obeyed them. Another point of resemblance between these two imposters is the eloquence with which both were endowed. The chronicles of Iceland represent Odin as one of the most persuasive of men. Nothing, say they, could resist the power of his discourses. Sometimes he mingled his harangues with the verses which he composed. Not only was he a great poet, but he was the first who inspired the Scandinavians with the charms of poetry. He was the inventor of *Runic* characters; but what most contributed to make him pass for a god, was the belief that he excelled in magic. It was believed that he could run over the universe in the twinkling of an eye; that he ruled the air and disposed of tempests; that he could raise the dead to life, predict future events, and transform himself at will; that, by the force of his enchantments, he took away the strength of his enemies, gave back health again to his friends, and discovered all treasures hidden under ground. These chronicles, more poetical than faithful, say, that he sung such melodious and tender airs, as to attract, by the sweetness of his songs, the spirits of the dead, who left their black abysses to come and range themselves around him.

His eloquence, together with his august and venerable air, caused him to be respected and revered in assemblies, whilst his bravery and skill in arms, rendered him formidable in battle. The terror, with which he inspired his enemies, was so great, that, in order to depict it, he was said to strike them deaf and blind. Like a desperate wolf, or an enraged lion, he rushed amidst the enemy's ranks, striking his buckler with fury, and spreading around him a horrible carnage, without ever receiving any wound. We must not forget, however, in reading these descriptions of his brilliant exploits, that the historians, who have transmitted them to us, were poets. Odin, carrying with him arts before unknown in the north, an extraordinary magnificence, a masterly address, and rare talents, could easily pass for a god in a country where nobody equalled him, and in which the people gave the name of prodigies to all at whose exploits they were greatly astonished.

GENERAL IDEA OF THE ANCIENT RELIGION OF NORTHERN EUROPE.

The Greek and Latin authors had but little intercourse with the northern people, whom they styled barbarians. They were ignorant even of their language, especially as the Celts made a scruple of unraveling to foreigners the thread of their doctrines. Hence, the former, compelled to remain spectators of their worship, could hardly seize the spirit of it. Yet, by gathering the traits preserved by those different writers, and by comparing them with the chronicles of the North, we hope to succeed in distinguishing the most important points.

The religion of the Scythians appears to have been simple in early times. It inculcated but few tenets, and was, in all probability, the only religion of the European aboriginals. It is generally remarked, that, under southerly climes, men are born with vivid, prolific, and restless imaginations, and are greedy for the marvellous; and that their ardent passions seldom allow them to keep up a just equilibrium. Hence, as soon as they leave the track of primitive traditions, they are apt to wander with a frightful rapidity. And hence arose the ravings of the priests among the Egyptians, Syrians, and, after them, the Greeks; and hence was produced that chaos, known by the name of mythology. In the north, on the contrary, religious opinions were less inconstant and fluctuating. There, the rigour of the climate chains the mind, checks the imagination, and curbs the passions; and man, obtaining nothing but by vigorous exertion, turns first upon objects of necessity, that activity which, under the torrid zone, is apt to run into the channels of inquietude and levity.

Notwithstanding this, the Scythians corrupted their worship by a mixture of ceremonies, some ridiculous, and others cruel. It becomes proper, therefore, to distinguish two ages in the religion of this people, and not confound the fictions of the poets with the creeds of their sages. This religion of the sages taught, that there was a *Supreme God, who was Ruler of the Universe*, to whom all were subject. And, according to Tacitus, such, also, was the god of the ancient Germans.

The ancient mythology of Iceland called God

the author of all that exists, the eternal, the ancient, the living, and the terrible being, the searcher into hidden things, the immutable. It attributed to this god, *omnipotence, omniscience, and incorruptible justice,* and forbade the representation of this divinity under any corporeal form. He could not be suitably regarded and adored but in the heart of retreats or in sacred forests. There he reigned in silence, and rendered himself sensible by the respect which he inspired. To represent him in a human figure, to attribute to him sex, to erect to him statues, justly appeared to these people an extravagant impiety. From this supreme divinity emanated a variety of subaltern genii, whose seat and temple was every thing in the visible world. These intelligences had the direction of its operations: the earth, water, fire, air, the moon, the stars, forests, rivers, mountains, lakes, winds, thunder, and tempests, received religious homage, which, at first, was directed only towards the intelligence that animated them. The motive of this worship was the fear of a God, offended by the sins of man, but merciful, and exorable to prayer and repentance. They addressed him as the active principle that produced all things, and as the only agent that preserved inferior beings, and dispensed events. To serve divinity by sacrifice and prayer, to do to others no wrong, to be brave and intrepid, were the chief moral consequences resulting from this worship. At length, the introduction of a life to come, cemented this religious edifice; cruel punishments were reserved for those who should have despised these three fundamental precepts, to continue as long as innumerable and endless delights were to reward the just, the religious, and the valiant.

Such are a few of the leading characteristics of that religion which, for several centuries, was adopted and practised by most people of Northern Europe, and, no doubt, by several Asiatic nations. It still preserved great purity towards the end of the Roman republic. The testimony of some authors proves that the ancient Germans had retained its principal tenets, while other nations, subdued and corrupted by the arms and luxury of the Romans, adopted their gods, and submitted to their yoke. We may, therefore, conclude, that it was at the time of Odin's arrival that this religion began to lose its primitive purity; as it is obvious, that this conqueror, by introducing himself to the people of the North as an awful divinity, had no other end than to secure dominion.

OF THE RELIGION OF NORTHERN EUROPE, SINCE ODIN.

The *Edda* of the Icelanders and their ancient poesies are the sole monuments which can give us any light on the ancient religion of the inhabitants of the north. From these sources we learn, that the most important alteration which it received after Odin, related to the number of the gods to be worshipped. The Scythians adopted, as the capital point of their religion, the adoration of one being, omnipotent and superior to all created intelligences. So reasonable a doctrine had so great influence over their minds, that they often displayed their contempt of the polytheism of those nations who treated them as barbarians; and every time they became the stronger party, their first care was to destroy all the objects of an idolatrous worship.

The fatal effects of example and of the times ultimately destroyed the simplicity of this religion; and the Scythians at last associated with the supreme god, subaltern divinities. Fear, desire, want, and passion, were the origin of this guilty change; and we are aware that the same causes have tended to corrupt all religions contrived by men. As those degenerate people began to think that one individual being could not watch over all parts of the universe, they considered it a duty to call to his aid, other minds, genii, and divinities of every description. But their predominant passions became the measure of their faith; wherefore the supreme god, the first idea of whom embraced all that exists, was only worshipped by the greater portion of the Scythians, as the god of war: than which rank, according to them, no honour could be more worthy of his attention, or better calculated to make his power conspicuous. Hence, those hideous pictures, which, in the Icelandic mythology, show us Odin as *the terrible and severe god, the father of carnage, the depopulator, the incendiary, the eagle, the blusterer, the donor of victory, the reriver of courage in combat, the namer of those who were to be killed.* Warriors going to fight vowed to send him a certain number of souls; which souls were the *right of Odin.* It was thought, that he often came into battle to inflame the fury of the combatants, to strike those whom he designed to perish, and to carry away souls to the celestial abodes.

Yet, according to the ancient Icelandic mythology, that terrible divinity, which took pleasure in shedding the blood of men, was the father and creator of them. *"God,* says the *"Edda",* sees and governs for centuries, directs all that is high and low, great and small. He made heaven, air, and man, who is to live forever; and before heaven and earth were made, this god was already with the giants."* It is likely that the ambitious Odin thus confounded and mixed up divers opinions, in order to consolidate the empire which he had usurped over men and over their minds. Some traces of the worship paid to him among the people of the North, still remain. The fourth day of the week still bears his name. It is called, according to different dialects, *Odensdag, Ousdag, Wodens-day,* and *Wednesday.* This god was also accounted the inventor of the arts; and is thought to correspond with the Mercury of the Greeks and Romans. The day sacred to Mercury was called *Dies Mercurii* (the day of Mercury.) The French call it *Mercredi.*

Odin was called Alfadur, (father of all,) because the gods were descended from him and his wife Frigga, or Walfadur, because he was the father of all who fell in battle. He had upwards of one hundred and twenty names.

The residence of the gods is Asgard, a fortress

whence the bridge Bifrost leads to the earth. Valaskialf was the silver palace of Odin. He sits upon the elevated throne Lidskjalf, whence he sees every thing in the universe. By his side stands the spear Gungner. His steed is called Sleipner. In the centre of Asgard, which is in the valley of Ida, was situated the place of meeting, the most splendidly ornamented of all, where the gods administered justice. Herein appeared Gladheim, the hall of joy, Wingolf, the palace of friendship and love, and Glasor, the forest of golden trees.

After Odin, the principal divinity of the north was Frigga or Frea, his wife. All the Celtic nation, the ancient Syrians, and the aboriginals of Greece, believed that the celestial god was connected with Earth, in order to produce by her subaltern deities, man, and all other creatures; and upon this belief was founded the veneration they had for Earth. They called her *mother earth, the mother of the gods*. The Phœnicians adored these two principles under the name of *Tautes* and *Astarte*. Some Scythian nations named them Jupiter and Apia; the Thracians, Cotis and Bendis; the Greeks and Romans, *Saturn* and *Ops*. The Scythians served Earth as a consort of the supreme god. Tacitus attributes the same worship to the ancient Germans, and especially to the inhabitants of Northern Germany. We cannot doubt that Hertus, or Earth, of whom he speaks, was the same as the *Frea* of the

Scandinavians. In the old Teutonic language, *Frea* or *Frau*, signifies a woman.

In succeeding times, this Frea became the goddess of love and debauchery, the Venus of the north, no doubt, because she was deemed the principle of all fecundity, and the mother of. all that exists. It was to her that they applied for marriage and happy deliveries. She dispensed pleasure, rest, voluptuousness. Frea shared with Odin the souls of those who were killed in war. The sixth day of the week was sacred to her under the name of *Freytag* (Friday,) and called by the Latins *Dies Veneris* (the day of Venus.) It is named *Vendredi* by the French.

The third among the principal divinities of the Scandinavians, was named Thor, the god of thunder — a symbol of physical strength. His mighty step sounded like the storm. His hammer, Miolner, (the Crusher,) crushed the hardest rocks. His son Uller, the beautiful god of archery and skating, was invoked by duellists. He had a silver circle round the down of his chin. His empire was called Ydalir (Rain-Valleys.) Julius Cesar expressly speaks of a god of the Gauls who presided over winds and tempests. He designates him by the Latin name of Jupiter; but Lucian gives him another name, which more nearly resembles that of Thor: he calls him *Taranis*, a name which, among the Gauls again signifies *thunder*. The authority of

Thor was extended to winds, seasons and thunderbolts. In the primitive system of the religion of the North, Thor was probably a subaltern divinity, born of the union of Odin with Earth. The Edda pronounces him the most valiant of the sons of Odin; and the club with which he is armed, and which he throws in the air at the giants, designates a thunderbolt. He was looked upon as the defender and avenger of the gods. Besides that club, which returned of itself to the hand that had hurled it, and which he grasped with iron gauntlets, he possessed a girdle which renewed strength in proportion as one needed it. It was with these dreadful arms that he fought the enemies of the gods.

The three divinities just named, composed the courts or supreme council of the gods. They were the principal objects of worship. But the Scandinavians did not all agree as to the one who should have the preference. The Danes particularly honored Odin; the Norwegians considered themselves under the safeguard of Thor; and the Swedes had for their tutelary god Freya, who, according to the *Edda*, presided over the seasons of the year, and gave fertility, riches, and peace.

The number and employment of the divinities of the second order are not easily determined. We shall merely give an outline.

The *Edda* enumerates twelve gods and twelve

goddesses, who received divine honors, but whose power was subordinate to that of Odin, the oldest of the gods, and the principle of all things. Such was Niord, the Neptune of the North, who was the god of winds, of sailors, of commerce, and of riches. He shook his vans in the roaring storm in such a manner as to make every thing tremble. By his wife Scala, daughter of the mountain Thiasse, he had the beautiful, beneficent, and mighty Frei and Freya. Frei, the ruler of the sun, dispenses rain and sunshine, plenty or dearth. He rides on a boar with golden bristles. The name, of his wife is Gerda, Gymer's daughter. The Celts placed Niord in the rank of inferior gods; but the importance and extent of his empire, caused him to be dreaded. The *Edda* devoutly recommends to adore him for fear that he would do evil. Wherefore temples were raised to his honor, for fear is the most superstitious of the passions.

Balder, son of Odin, was another god. He was the youthful, beautiful, and wise god of eloquence and of just decision. He appeared as brilliant in innocence as the lily, and the whitest flower was hence called Baldrian. He was endued with so great majesty, that his looks were resplendent. He was the sun of the Celts, the same as the Grecian Apollo. His wife Nanna regarded her husband with modest admiration and affectionate enthusiasm. She brought him Forfete, who was the god of concord, and who had a palace, called Glitner, supported by pillars.

Tyr, whom we must distinguish from Thor, was the god of power and valour, and the patron of brave warriors and athletes. He wounded by a look, was lofty as a fir, and brandished the lightnings of battle. Brage was the god of eloquence, wisdom, and poetry, which, from him, is called Bragur. He had a golden telyn, and swept the cords, which emitted a sweet sound. His wife *Iduna*, the goddess of youth, had charge of certain apples, of which the gods ate when they felt the approach of old age, and the power of which was to make them grow young again. Hiemdal, a son of nine gigantic sisters, born on the margin of the earth, was their door keeper. He appeared with a pensive brow, and his eyes cast down. The rainbow (Bifrost) was the bridge, communicating from heaven to earth. Hiemdal watched over its extremities to prevent the giants from scaling heaven. He slept as lightly as birds; and day and night, he perceived objects at more than a hundred leagues distant. He heard the grass and the wool of sheep grow; and held in one hand a sword, and in the other, a trumpet, the noise of which was heard in all worlds. Hermode, the messenger of the gods, was armed with a helmet and mail. Vidar, the god of silence, was as strong as Thor, and walked the waters and the air. Hoder, the blind god, was the murderer of Balder. The gods never forgot his violent actions, and would not hear his name pronounced. Wale was the formidable god of the bow. The Scandinavians gave to the bad principle the name of *Loke*, and placed it in the number of their gods. He was the son of the giant Farbaute and of Laufeya. He is, says the *Edda*, "*the calumniator of the gods, the artificer of frauds, the opprobrium of the gods and of men. He is beautiful of body, but malignant of spirit, and inconstant in his inclinations; none among mortals surpass him in the art of perfidy and of cunning*". He had several children of *Signie*, his wife. Three monsters also owed their existence to him: the wolf *Fenris*, the serpent *Migdard*, and *Hela* or death, all being enemies of the gods, who, after divers efforts, inclosed the wolf Fenris, where he is to remain until the last day, when he will be let loose, and devour the sun. The serpent was cast into the sea, where he will remain until conquered by the god Thor; and Hela was banished into the infernal abodes, where she has the government of nine worlds, which she divides among those who are sent to her. Loke was locked up by the gods in a cave shut by three sharp stones, where he shudders with such rage, as to cause the earthquakes. He will remain there captive until the end of time, and then be killed by Hiemdal, door-keeper to the gods.

The Icelandic Mythology counted twelve goddesses, at the head of whom was Frea or Frigga, the consort of Odin. Each of them had her peculiar offices. Eira was the goddess of medicine; Gelione, of virginity; she protects chaste females, and, if they die unmarried, takes them to her heavenly dwellings; lyna, the goddess of friendship and good faith, kisses away the tear from the eye of the unfortunate; Siona excites good feelings in the bosoms of youth, and especially maidens, and disposes them to mutual love; Fulla, a virgin with beautiful locks, and wearing a diadem of gold, was the confident of Frigga, and the patroness of finery; Freya, the goddess of lovers, is the most mild and bountiful of the divinities. Her eye is an eternal spring; her neck and cheeks, light itself. She encourages sweet songs, and listens to the prayers of mortals. More faithful than Venus, she incessantly weeps over her absent husband Odrus; (to whom she bore two daughters, Nossa, the model of all beauty and grace, and Gersemi;) but her tears are drops of gold. Lofna reconciles divided consorts. Vara receives their oath, and punishes those who violate them. *Snotra*, the goddess of modesty, sciences, and good morals, patronises virtuous youths and maidens. Gna, the messenger of Frea, floats about with the rays of the sun; Synia, the guard of heaven, protects justice and law, avenges broken faith, and exposes perjury; *Wora*, the omniscient goddess, penetrates every secret of the heart; and *Saga* presides over waterfalls.

Besides these twelve goddesses, there are other virgins in *Valhalla*, or the paradise of heroes. They are majestic and beautiful, neither daughters of heaven, nor born in hell; neither begotten by gods, nor acknowledged by immortal mothers; and are named the *Valkyrias*, or *Disas*. They appear with a helmet and mail, and mounted on swift horses. It is their duty to wait upon heroes. Odin also employs them in fights, to choose out those who were doomed to destruction, and to incline the victory to the side he pleases; for these courageous people took care not to attribute defeats to their weakness, or want of valour; but these, as well as victory, were attributed solely to the will of Odin.

> *"On steeds that seem'd as fleet as light,*
> *Six maids in brilliant armour dight,*
> *Their chargers of ethereal birth,*
> *Paw'd, with impatient hoof, the earth,*
> *And snorting fiercely 'gan to neigh,*
> *As if they heard the battle bray,*
> *And burn'd to join the bloody fray.*
> *But they unmov'd and silent sate,*
> *With pensive brow and look sedate,*

Proudly each couch'd her glittering
    spear,
And seem'd to know nor hope nor fear.
    So mildly firm their placid air,
    So resolute, yet heav'nly fair.
But not one ray of pity's beam,
From their dark eyelids seem'd to gleam;
Nor gentle mercy's melting tear,
Nor love might ever harbour there. .
Was never woman's beauteous face,
So stern, and yet so passionless."

— HELGA.

The court of the gods was usually held under a large oak, where they administered justice. This oak is represented as the largest of all trees Its branches covered the surface of the world, and its top reached to the heavens. It was supported by three large roots, one of which extended even to the ninth world, or to hell. On its branches sat an eagle, whose piercing eye surveyed the whole universe. A squirrel (Rotatoskr) ran up and down the oak to make his reports; four stags (Dain, Dynais, Dnalion, and Dryathor) roamed through its branches; several serpents twined around its trunk, and strove to destroy it; and in a neighbouring spring, called the *fountain of past things*, three virgins continually drew a kind of precious water, with which they watered the tree. This water keeps up the beauty of its leaves, and after having refreshed its branches, it falls back on the ground, where it keeps up the dew with which bees compose their honey. The three beautiful virgins, the *Nornas*, often meet under the oak, where they determine the fate of mortals. Their names are *Urd*, (the Past,) *Varande*, (the Present,) and *Skuld*, (the Future.)

Such were the principal divinities of the North, or, rather, the ideas which the poets gave of them to the credulous. It was by fictions, sometimes ingenious, that they endeavoured to extol the simplicity of their religion; but various passages in ancient history, show that many did not follow this creed, acknowledging no other subaltern divinity than their own courage.

Having thus enumerated the names and attributes of the principal gods, we will now proceed to set forth some of the tenets of the Celtic religion: and, first, we will notice those in the *Edda*, and in the poem, called *Volupsa*. It is thought that the latter was composed by Sæmond, surnamed the Learned. Several fragments of the *first Edda* are still extant. The most valuable is the poem entitled *Volupsa*, i. e. *Oracle of the Prophetess*. It contains about four hundred verses, and includes an abridgment of the whole Mythology of the North.

That portion of it which the Mythology of Iceland has preserved, deserves the more attention, as, in disclosing to us the sentiments of the ancient Celts on this important point, it is sometimes expressed in a style of sublime elevation.

The reader can judge for himself of the resemblance it bears to sacred tradition.

In the dawn of time, says the poet, there was neither sea, river, nor refreshing zephyr. Neither heaven above, nor earth below, was seen; all was nothing but a vast, herbless, and seedless abyss, (Nislheim,) in which flowed the fountain, (Hwergelmer,) swallowing up every thing with twelve rivers (Eliwagar issuing from this fountain.) The sun had no palace; the stars did not know their homes; the moon did not know her power. Then there appeared a luminous, burning, and an inflamed world on the side of the south (Musspellheim;) and from this burning world, there incessantly slide away into the abyss, (which was in the north,) torrents of sparkling fire, which, in falling, were congealed into the abyss, and filled it up with scoria and ice. Thus the abyss was heaped up, little by little; but there remained within a light and immovable air, and frozen vapours were incessantly exhaled, until a breath of heat, being sent from the south, melted those vapours, and formed living drops, whence sprang the giant Ymer. It is related that, while he was sleeping, he formed of his perspiration, a male and a female, from whom was descended the race of giants; a race as vile and corrupt as Ymer its author. By the mixture of ice and heat was produced the cow (Audumbla,) from whose dugs flowed four streams of milk, on which Ymer lived. The cow fed on the salt stones, which she was one day licking, when, in the evening, human hair grew out of them. On the next day appeared a head; and on the third, an entire man, called *Bure*. His son *Bor* married Belsta, daughter of the giant Mountain-Gate. By her he had three sons, Odin, Wile, and Ve. There arose a better race, that was connected with that of the giant Ymer. It was called the family of Bor, from the name of the first of that family, who was father to Odin. The sons of Bor killed the giant Ymer, and the blood flowed from his wound in so great abundance, that it caused a general inundation, in which all the giants except one, perished. He being saved by means of a boat, escaped with his whole family. Then a new world was formed. The sons of Bor, or the gods, hurried the body of the giant into the abyss, and out of him fabricated the globe. With his blood they formed the sea and the rivers; the earth, with his flesh; large mountains, with his bones; rocks, with his teeth, and the fragments of his broken bones. They made of his skull the arch of heaven, which is sustained by four dwarfs, named South, (Sudre,) North, (Nordure,) East, (Austere,) and West,

(Westre.) They threw his brain into the air, and it formed the clouds. They there placed flambeaux to enlighten it, and fixed to other fires the space which they were to survey; some in heaven, others under heaven. Days were distinguished, and years had their number. They made the earth round, and girded it with the deep Ocean, on the shores of which they placed giants. One day as the sons of Bor, or the gods, walked there, they found two floating pieces of wood, out of which they formed man and woman. The elder of the sons gave them soul and life; the second, motion and science; the third endowed them with speech, hearing, and sight, to which he added beauty and dress. It is from this man, named *Askus*, (Ash,) and from this woman, named *Embla*, (Alder,) that is descended the race of men, which now inhabit the earth.

The giant Narfi (darkness) had a daughter named Nott, (night.) She was thrice married. By her husband Nagelfari, (air, ether) she had a son, Andur, (matter;) by Anar, (the forming principle,) Jord, (the earth;) by Dellinger, (twilight,) Dagur, (day.) Alfadur transported Nott and Dagur to the heavens, and furnished them each with a horse and chariot, to drive round the earth daily. Nott was first drawn by her horse Hrimfaxi, (black-mane,) which every morning bedews the earth with the foam from his mouth. The horse of

Dagur, Skinfaxi, (shining mane,) illuminates the world with his manes. Mundelfari (the mover of the axis,) had two beautiful children, Sool (sun,) and Maan (moon.) He married his daughter to Glemur, the god of joy. Disapproving of his presumptuous conduct, the gods carried away his children, and took them up to the heavens. They were employed in driving the chariots of the sun and moon.

We may easily recognize in the foregoing narration, the vestiges of a general tradition, the various circumstances of which most nations have embellished, altered, or suppressed at pleasure. If we compare it, together with the traditions of the Chaldeans, Syrians, and Egyptians, the theogony of Hesiod, and with the mythology of the Greeks and Romans, we shall doubtless be convinced, That the conformity which is found between the leading circumstances of these accounts and that given in *Genesis*, cannot be the effect of mere chance.

The description of chaos given in the *Edda*; that quickening breath which produced the great giant Ymer; that sleep, during which a man and a woman were born of his sides; that race of the sons of the gods; that deluge from which one man alone escaped with his family in a boat; that renewing of the world which followed the deluge; that first man, that first woman, created by the gods, and who received motion from them: all this can be nothing but the vestiges and recollections of a general and more ancient creed. We recognize in these altered accounts, the same allegories, the same fictions, the same desire of explaining the phenomena of nature, which have decked out fables among all people. In considering the style of these fables, in which are blended, sometimes the sublime, with the peurile, sometimes littleness placed amidst the most magnificent pictures, the disorder of narration, and the uniform turn of idea and expression, we cannot but discover evident marks of a high antiquity, and the manner of expression peculiar to a simple, primitive people, whose vigorous imagination, despising or not familiar with rules, is displayed with all the liberty and all the energy of nature.

According to the Celts, matter already existing, but without form and life, was animated and disposed by the gods in the order which we now admire it. No heathen religion has granted more than that of the Celts to divine providence. This tenet was for them the key of all the phenomena of nature, without exception. All bodies and beings acted up to the influence of subaltern intelligences, who were themselves merely the organs and instruments of the divine will. Hence, that error common to so many nations, which caused the trembling of leaves, the crackling of flame, the roar of thunder, the flight or song of birds, the involuntary emotions of men, dreams and visions, and the like, to be looked upon as instructions or inspirations of the Supreme Being. Hence, too, are oracles, divinations, soothsayers, lots, augurs, presages, and illusions, brought forth by the inquietude and weakness of men. By admitting the immediate and continual influence of divinity over all creatures, the Celts considered it impossible for man to change the course of things, or to resist the destinies.

We have already seen that they admitted three Fairies or Nornas, who determined all events. Every man had a fairy, who was present at his birth, watched over his actions, and, beforehand, marked out all the events of his life and the limit of his days. It is to that tenet of the Celtic mythology that the fables of fairy-ism and the marvellous of our Gothic romances may be attributed, although the mythology of the Greeks and Romans assisted in the embellishment of their fictions, their poems, and their romances. We may easily conceive how much a belief in predestination was calculated to add to the temerity of the most warlike people on earth. The inhabitants of the North joined to this doctrine a still more barbarous and dangerous prejudice, namely; they believed that the limit of the life of a man could be put forward if some one should die for him. When some celebrated warrior or some prince was about to perish, it was thought that Odin, appeased by the sacrifice of another victim, repealed the decree, and prolonged the days of him whom that victim would save.

The precepts of the Celtic religion were chiefly confined to their being intrepid in war, to their serving the gods, and appeasing them by sacrifices, to their being just, hospitable to strangers, faithful to their word, and true to their conjugal faith.

TENETS OF THE CELTS IN REFERENCE TO THE FUTURE STATE, AND TO THE LAST DESTINIES OF THIS WORLD.

There will come a time, says the *Edda*, a barbarous age, a sword age, when crimes will infest the earth, when the brothers will wallow in the blood of their brethren, when the sons will be the assassins of their fathers, and the fathers of their children, and no one will spare his friend. Soon after a grievous winter will happen; the snow will fall from the four corners of the world; the winds will blow furiously; the frost will harden the earth; and three such winters will follow in succession. Then there will appear astonishing prodigies; monsters will break their chains and escape; the great dragon will roll in the ocean, and by his motions the earth will be overflown; the trees will be rooted up; the rocks will be rent; the wolf Fenris, unchained, will open his enormous jaws which will reach from earth to heaven; fire will issue from his nostrils and eyes; he will devour the sun, and the great dragon who follows him, will vomit upon the waters and in the air, torrents of venom. In this confusion the stars will flee away, the heaven will be split, and an army of evil genii and of giants, conducted by their princes, will enter to attack the gods; but Hiendal, the door-keeper of the gods, will arise and blow his roaring trumpet; the gods will awake and meet again; the great oak will shake its branches; and heaven and earth will be full of fear. The gods will arm, and the heroes take sides in battle. Odin will appear, clothed with his golden helmet and his resplendent cuirass; and with his broad cymeter in his hand, attack the wolf Fenris, which will devour him, and both perish together. Thor will be smothered in the torrents of vemon which the dragon will emit while dying. The fire will consume all, and the flame rise to heaven; but soon a new earth will emerge from the bosom of the waves, adorned with green meadows. The fields will then produce abundant harvests without culture; calamities will be unknown. Lift and Liftrasor, a human pair saved from the destruction, and fed with morning dew, will renew the human race.

There will be an elevated palace in it, covered with gold, and more brilliant than the sun, and there the just will dwell and rejoice for centuries. Then the powerful and the valiant, and he who governs all, will come from the abodes on high to administer divine justice, pronounce decrees, and establish the sacred destinies which will always last. Widar, (the conqueror,) and Wale, (the powerful,) will remain with the gods. Mode, (mental power,) and Magne, (strength,) will receive the crushing hammer when Thor is killed, and Widar will tear the jaws of the wolf asunder. There will be an abode remote from the sun, with doors turned towards the north. In it poison will rain through a thousand gaps. It will be composed of the carcasses of serpents. Torrents will flow there, in which will be plunged perjurers, assassins, and those who seduce married women. A black winged dragon will incessantly hover about, and devour the bodies of the unhappy who are shut up therein.

Notwithstanding the obscurity which pervades these descriptions, we see by them that the Scandinavians held as a doctrine of their religion, the immortality of the soul, and future rewards and punishments. This idea was general among the Celts; and upon it they founded the obligation to serve the gods, and to be brave in battle. Were it not for that monument of the Icelandic mythology, which we have referred to, we should know but little of the religion of our forefathers.

The Iceland mythology expressly distinguishes two different abodes for the happy, and as many for the guilty.

The first was the palace of Odin, called *Valhalla*, where that god received all who died a violent death, from the beginning of the world down to that general downfall of nature, which was to be followed by a second generation.

The second was the palace covered with gold, where the just were to rejoice eternally after the renewing of all things. In regard to the places of punishment, two were likewise distinguished. One of which, called N*islheim*, was to last only until the end of the world; and the other, called *Nastroud*, was to be eternal. The first two future abodes seemed to be intended rather to reward courage and violence than virtue. Those only who died in battle, had a right to the happiness which Odin prepared in the Valhalla. All wounds received in battle, were there healed by the trumpet's sounding for the feast; and then the heroes quaffed the oil of Enherium, and the Valkyrias filled their cups. All who died not imbrued with blood, had the fear of entering into Nislheim, a mansion composed of nine worlds, and reserved principally for those who should die of sickness or old age. Hela or Death there exercised her empire; her palace was Grief (Elidnir;) her table, Hunger (Hungr;) her servants, Lethargy (Ganglati,) and

Delay (Ganghol;) the threshold of her door. Precipice; her bed, Disease (Kor;) and her looks froze with affright. The dog of darkness, resembling the Grecian Cerberus, guarded the entrance of Nislheim.

From the foregoing account it would seem, that the Scandinavians and the people of the north made war their chief occupation, and carried valour even to the excess of fanaticism.

> *"Uprose the king of men with speed,*
> *And saddled strait, his coal-black steed;*
> *Down the yawning steep he rode,*
> *That leads to Hela's drear abode.*
> *Him the dog of darkness spied;*
> *His shaggy throat he opened wide,*
> *While from his jaws with carnage fill'd,*
> *Foam and human gore distill'd.*
> *Hoarse he bays, with hideous din,*
> *Eyes that glow and fangs that grin."*

— GRAY'S DESCENT OF ODIN.

Valva.

> *"Hard by the eastern gate of hell*
> *In ancient time great Valva fell;*
> *And there she lies in massive tomb,*

Shrouded by night's eternal gloom.
Fairer than gods, and wiser, she
Held the strange keys of destiny,
Ere world there was, or gods, or man;
No mortal tongue has ever said,
What hand unknown laid Valva dead.
But yet if rumour rightly tells,
In her cold bones the spirit dwells;
And still if bold intruder come,
Her voice unfolds his hidden doom,
And oft the rugged ear of hell
Is sooth'd by some melodious spell,
Slow breathing from the hollow stone
In witching notes and solemn tone."

— HERBERT'S HELGA.

The Song of Valva.

"Silence, all ye sons of glory!
   Silence, all ye powers of light!
While I sing of ancient story,
   Wonders wrapt in mystic night.

I was rock'd in giants' cradle,
   Giants' lore my wisdom gave;
I have known both good and evil,
   Now I lie in lowly grave.

Long before the birth of Odin,
   Mute was thunderous ocean's roar;
Stillness o'er the huge earth brooding,
   Strand was none, nor rocky shore.

Neither grass nor green tree growing,
   Vernal shower, nor wintry storm;
Nor those horses, bright and glowing,
   Dragg'd the Sun's refulgent form.

He who rules, by night, the heaven,
   Wist not where his beams to throw;
All to barren darkness given,
   There, confusion; hell below.

Imir sate in lonely sadness,
   Watching o'er the fruitless globe;
Never morning beam'd with gladness;
   Never eve, with dewy robe.

Who are those in pride advancing,
   Through the barren tract of night?
Mark their steel divinely glancing, .
   Imir falls in holy fight!

Of his bones, the rocks high swelling,
   Of his flesh the glebe is made;
From his veins the tide is swelling,
   And his locks are verdant shade.

Hark! his crest with gold adorning,
  Chanticleer on Odin calls.
Hark! another bird of morning,
  Claps his wings in Hela's halls,

Nature shines in glory beaming;
  Elves are born, and man is form'd;
Ev'ry hill with gladness teeming,
  Ev'ry shape with life is warm'd.

Who is he by heav'n's high portal,
  Beaming like the light of morn?
'Tis Heimdallar's form immortal,
  Shrill resounds his golden horn.

Say, proud Warder, rob'd in glory,
  Are the foes of nature nigh?
Have they climb'd the mountains
    hoary?
  Have they storm'd the lofty sky?

On the wings of tempest riding,
  Surtur spreads his fiery spell;
Elves in secret caves are hiding;
  Odin meets the wolf of hell.

She must taste a second sorrow,
  She who wept when Balder bled;
Fate demands a nobler quarry;

Death must light on Odin's head.

See ye not yon silent stranger?
  Proud he moves with low'ring eyes,
Odin, mark thy stern avenger!
  Slain the shaggy monster lies.

See the serpent weakly crawling,
  Thor has bruis'd its loathsome head;
Lo! the stars from heav'n are falling!
  Earth has sunk in ocean's bed!

Glorious Sun, thy beams are shrouded,
  Vapours dark around thee sail;
Nature's eye with mists is clouded,
  Shall the powers of ill prevail?

Say, shall earth with freshness teeming,
  Once again from ocean rise?
Shall the dawn of glory streaming,
  Wake us to immortal joys?

He shall come in might eternal,
  He whom eye hath never seen;
Earth and heav'n and powers infernal,
  Mark his port and awful mien.

He shall judge, and he shall sever,
  Shame from glory, ill from good;

These shall live in light for ever,
  Those shall wade the chilling flood.

Dark to dwell in wo repining,
  Far beyond the path of day;
In that bower where serpents twining,
  Loathsome spit their venom'd spray."

— HERBERT'S HELGA.

PROGRESS OF THE RELIGION OF THE PEOPLE OF THE NORTH.

The Celtic religion generally taught that it was offending the gods to pretend to lock them up in an inclosure of walls. In Denmark, in Sweden, and in Norway, amidst plains and on hills, are still found altars about which they assembled for sacrifices and other religious ceremonies. Three large rocks raised upon the summit of a small hill, serve as a basis to a large flat stone, under which is ordinarily a cavity, which probably served to receive the blood of victims. Firestones were commonly found, for no fire except that of their altars, was considered pure enough for so holy a purpose. Sometimes these altars were constructed with more elegance, greater regularity, and nicer proportions. In Selande one still remains, the stones of which are of a prodigious size. Even at this day, men might well hesitate to undertake a similar work, although with the advantage over its original builders, of the powerful aid of machinery. What increases our astonishment is, that the stones of which this structure is composed, are very rare in the isle of Selande; for which reason they must have been transported a great distance — monuments more lasting than any of modern art or industry. At all times, men have thought that in order to honour deity more highly, they ought to make for him some prodigious efforts, and to consecrate to him their riches. Europe and Asia lavished their treasures to construct the temple at Ephesus. The people of the North, whose strength, courage, patience, and perseverance, constituted their sole riches, bore heavy masses of rocks on to the tops of hills. In some places in Norway, are also found grottoes cut in the rock with wonderful patience, and intended for religious purposes.

In proportion as the people of the North formed new alliances with other nations, their religion underwent alterations; step by step new temples were raised, and new idols were adopted. The three principal tribes or hordes of Scandinavia, erected temples to Envy; but none, it is said, was more famous than that at Upsal in Sweden. Gold there glittered on every side. A chain of that metal surrounded the roof, though its circumference was nine hundred ells. Haquin, count of Norway, had built one near Drontheim, almost equal to that of Upsal. When Olaus, king of Norway, embraced the Christian faith, he caused that temple and its idols to be razed and broken. There were found in it immense riches; and among other things, a very costly golden ring.

Iceland had also its temples. The chronicles mention two that were highly celebrated, situated, the one in the north, the other in the south of the island. In each of these temples, says an author of that country, was a particular chapel, or sacred woody place. It was there that idols were placed upon an altar, around which were ranged the victims that were to be immolated; and near the chapel there was a deep well, into which victims were thrown headlong.

All these temples were razed when Denmark embraced Christianity, and the very remembrance of the places which they occupied, is lost; but some tables of altars, dispersed in the woods and on the mountains, still testify that the ancient Danes were no less attached to that worship than the other nations of the North.

The large temple at Upsal seemed to be particularly consecrated to the three great divinities. They were there represented by their peculiar symbols. Odin held a sword in his hand. Thor, on the left of Odin, had a crown on his head, a sceptre in one hand, and a club in the other. Sometimes he was represented in a chariot drawn by two wooden he-goats, with a silver bridle, and his head crowned with stars. Frigga, on the left of Thor, was represented with various attributes, among which the goddess of pleasure might be recognized.

Odin was honored as the god of battle and of victory; Thor, as the ruler of the seasons, and dispenser of rain, drought, and fertility; Frigga, as the goddess of love and marriage.

They held three great festivals in the year. The first was celebrated at the winter solstice. The night was called the *night-mother*, being that which produced all others. This epoch also marked the beginning of their year, which, among the people of the North generally, was computed from one winter solstice to the other. This feast, the most solemn of all, was called *Juul*, and was celebrated in honor of Thor or of the sun, to obtain a fertile year. During its continuance, like the Roman Saturnalia, marks of the most dissolute joy were allowed. The second feast was instituted in honour of Earth or of the goddess Frigga. Pleasures, fecundity, and victory, were invoked. It was placed in the crescent of the second moon of the year.

The third feast, in honor of Odin, was celebrated with a great deal of elact at the commencement of spring; at which time they asked of that god, much fighting and success in projected enterprizes.

In early times, their offerings were simple, such as a pastoral people could afford. The first fruits of crops, and the most beautiful fruits of the earth, covered the altars of the gods. But in process of time, animals came to be immolated. To Thor were offered fattened horses and oxen; to Frigga, the largest hog that could be found; and to Odin, horses, dogs, and sometimes cocks and a fat bull.

When it was once laid down as a principle, that the effusion of the blood of animals appeased the wrath of the gods, and averted the strokes intended for the punishment of the guilty, sacrifices were rapidly multiplied; and in public calamities, that blood appearing too vile, they caused that of man to flow. This barbarous and almost universal usage has been traced to the highest antiquity; but the northern nations preserved it until the ninth century, because it was not until that period that they received the lights of Christianity, and the arts which had softened the manners of the Greeks, and Romans. The people of the North believed that the number three was cherished by the gods. Every ninth month or three times three, great sacrifices were renewed. They lasted nine days; and nine victims, either men or animals, were immolated. But the most solemn sacrifices were those which were made at Upsal every ninth year. Then, the king, the senate, and all distinguished individuals, were present, and brought their offerings which were placed in the large temple. The absent sent their presents, and the priests were charged to receive them. Strangers assembled in crowds. The access was shut to those who had lost their honor by some blemish, and especially to all who had lost their courage.

In time of war, they chose their human victims among captives; and in peace, among criminals. Nine persons were immolated; the will of the assembly and the lot combined, regulated this choice. The unfortunate upon whom the lot fell, were treated with so many honors and caresses by the assembly, and had so many promises of life to come, that they sometimes congratulated themselves on their destiny. The choice did not always fall on those of vile blood; for the more dear and noble the victim, the more highly they imagined they redeemed the divine benevolence. The history of the North teems with examples of kings and other fathers who imposed silence on nature in order to obey this barbarous custom.

When the victim was chosen, it was conducted towards the altar, where the sacred fire was burning day and night. Among the vessels of iron and copper employed one greater than the rest, served to receive the blood of victims. After having killed the animals, they opened their entrails to read futurity in them; and afterwards roasted the flesh, which was distributed in the assembly. When they immolated men, the victim was laid upon a large stone, where he was either choked or crushed. When the blood spouted with great impetuosity, it was considered one of the most favorable omens. The sad remains of human victims sacrificed, were either burned or suspended in a sacred wood near the temple. The blood was sprinkled partly upon the people, and partly upon the sacred wood. With it, they also besmeared the images of the gods, the altars, the benches, and the walls of the temple both within and without. Near the temple was a well, or deep spring, into which they sometimes cast a victim devoted to Frigga, the goddess of the earth. If it went quickly to the bottom she was pleased, and graciously received it. On the contrary, if it floated, she refused it, and it was suspended in the sacred forest. Near the temple of Upsal was a wood of this kind, every tree and leaf of which was looked upon as most holy. This wood, called Odin's, was filled up with bodies of men and of animals that had been sacrificed. They were sometimes carried off and buried in honor of Thor, or the sun; and when the smoke arose quickly, the people doubted not but these offerings had been most agreeable to him. When they immolated a victim, the priest said: *I devote thee to Odin, I send thee to Odin, or, I devote thee for a good crop, or, for the return of a good season.* The ceremony was terminated by feasts, in which was displayed all the magnificence known in that age. The kings and chief lords first gave toasts or salutes in honor of the gods; after which each one drank whilst making his prayer or vow.

Whatever horror we may now have for human sacrifices, it nevertheless appears by history, that this barbarous usage was once almost general on earth. The Gauls long offered men to their supreme god, Esus or Teutal. The aboriginals of Sicily and Italy, the Britons, the Phœnicians, the Carthaginians, and, indeed, almost all the nations of Europe and Asia, have been covered with the same opprobrium. The Peruvians and the Mexicans likewise offered human sacrifices. The latter once immolated, on a single occasion, five thousand prisoners of war. The wandering people of Africa and of America, again, gave themselves up to this guilty folly. But we cease to wonder at it, when we consider how liable ignorant nations are to fall into error. Man is surrounded with dangers and evils from his birth; and if the protection of laws and the enlightening aid of science, religion, and the arts, do not soften his passions, and encourage him to tread in the path of virtue in the morning of life; if they do not sweeten his temper, and spread over his soul that quietness and moderation which cause the social and kindlier affections to spring up, he is soon surrounded with a thousand black cares and terrors, which make him ferocious and distrustful. All those beings who share his wants, become his ideal enemies. Hence arises that thirst for revenge, and that eagerness for the destruction of his fellow man, which cannot be quenched whilst he entertains no respect for justice, nor for the sacred rights of others: and hence too, those impious prejudices, and dark conceptions which make men imagine sanguinary gods like themselves. Hence, those bloody rites which plunge the blade into the breast of the unfortunate victim of superstition, whilst pleading for his life, after having been stripped, by crime and force, from all other rights.

The same spirit of inquietude which induced the people of Asia and Greece, to seek all available means to penetrate into the secrets of futurity, operated with no less power upon the people of the North. In studying carefully the phenomena of nature, or rather, what *they* considered as the visible operations of a deity, they hoped to succeed in ascertaining his tastes, inclinations, and will. Oracles, augurs, divinations, and a thousand of the like practices followed.

The three Parcæ whom we have mentioned, delivered oracles in temples. That of Upsal was the most celebrated, on account of its replies, as well as its sacrifices.

It was generally thought, that some diviners had familiar spirits, which did'not leave them, and which they could consult, under the form of small idols. It was also believed, that others conjured the manes from their tombs, and forced them to relate the destinies. Odin gave out, that he had this power; an ancient Icelandic ode describes him as descending into hell, where he consults a celebrated prophetess.

Ignorance, which caused poetry to be considered as supernatural, caused the belief, that the Runic characters or letters contained mysterious and magic virtues. Odin, who was looked upon as the inventor of these characters, asserted that, by their means, he could raise the dead to life.

There were Runic letters appropriated to obtain victory, to cure the evils of the body, and to dissipate sorrow. The same characters were employed in all the different cases; but their combination, and the manner of tracing them, were varied. Sometimes it was from the right to the left, or from the left to the right; now from the top to the bottom, and then in a circle, or against the course of the sun.

We shall not dwell upon the mortifying spectacle of the credulity, ignorance, and errors of men. What we have related, is sufficient to show how necessary it is that they should be guided by lights superior to those of their reason.

RESEARCHES INTO THE ANCIENT RELIGION OF THE PRIMITIVE INHABITANTS OF GREAT BRITAIN.

During the infancy of states, as during that of men, shining actions are rare: the arts and sciences do not arise but in succeeding ages. Historians do not exist, but among already civilized nations; and hence, the few facts of early ages that come to us, are the exaggerated and altered accounts handed down by uncertain tradition.

We have already observed, that most nations give for their founders, either gods or imaginary heroes. We have shown that the Greeks made similar exertions to veil their real origin; but that their fables, which were a fantastical admixture of real remembrances and of the flights of imagination, become records which, to no small extent, depose in favour of truth.

The *name* of a god often appears to be that of a sage, sometimes designated by a word taken from a foreign language; and these etymologies are the traces which truth leaves behind her, and which all the exertions of self-love cannot efface.

In the general view, by which we have attempted to trace out the origin of idolatry and the history of mythology, it evidently appears, that it is to the Oriental countries we must look, if we wish to find the cradle of the human race. The more we search into history, the more clearly it appears that those rich and flourishing countries were the native soil of our first parents; and that they were also the brilliant centre whence the arts and sciences irradiated spread over the rest of the world.

It would be difficult, perhaps even impossible, to ascertain how, and at what precise time, the British isles became inhabited. The study of natural history induces us to believe, that they formerly made a part of the European continent; but neither the memory nor the monuments of men have preserved any record which might indicate the period of their separation. It is well enough to extend our observations to those ages and early histories which have left some vestiges, where the mind can walk without being swallowed up in useless and audacious speculations and imaginings. But human vanity will in vain attempt to roll back the current of time; whose longest period will be but an imperceptible point in eternity which precedes and follows it.

Without pretending to indicate the time in which England was first peopled, it is probable that Gaul was inhabited before it was. It is natural to suppose that men ventured through the seas in order to fix themselves in the isles, only when they had become somewhat populous.

We know that the Celts were once the masters of Europe, from the mouth of the Obi in Russia to Cape Finisterre. The same language having been adopted among those nations separated from each other by immense forests is the only monument which remains to us to point out that fact; but it throws no light on the beginning of their history.

The most renowned of all the Celts, are those who inhabited Gaul; and it is to the historians of the nations against whom they carried on frequent wars, that they owe their celebrity. Julius Cesar and Tacitus relate that Great Britain was the first country which the Celtic Gauls peopled.

The relative situation of those countries renders their statement probable; and the conformity of language and of customs which existed between the Britons and the Gauls, leaves no doubt of their having had a common origin. It appears that the Gallic colony at first settled in that portion of the island which is opposite to Gaul. They then extended towards the north, and gradually peopled the whole island.

Whatever may have been the origin of the inhabitants of Great Britain, they were numerous enough, and, above all, courageous enough, to resist the Romans, who were then masters of the known world.

Their government was at that time a mixture of monarchy and aristocracy. The chiefs watched over the execution of the laws; but the legislative power was vested in the hands of the druids. The people regarded as the infallible organs of divinity, those pontiffs so celebrated by their divination, and that of their wives, by their pretended intercourse with heaven, and by their manner of living, which was as austere as retired. It was by the influence of those supreme pontiffs, that the nation united under one chief, whose magistracy, resembling the Roman dictatorship, was not to last longer than during the time necessary to terminate wars, and remove dangers.

The druids long preserved that high authority among the Celts, especially in Great Britain; but, after the beginning of the second century, their credit decreased, because wars were multiplied, and the nobility, hurried away by its bloody carnage, no more pressed so many to enter into that order. The number of priests accordingly diminished; and the precepts of religion were soon altered and almost forgotten in the tumults of camps.

Victory favouring those of the chiefs who were called *Vergobrets*, (a title equal to that of *kings*,) rendered their power more independent of the druids. Tremnor, great-grandfather to the celebrated Fingal, had been elected vergobert by the victorious tribes that he had conducted to victory. The druids were deputed to him to order him to resign his power. The refusal of Tremnor caused a civil war, in which a very large number of druids perished. Those who escaped the carnage, hid themselves in the heart of forests and in caves, where they devoted themselves to meditation; and the vergobrets or kings seized the whole authority.

In the meantime, in order to strengthen their power, to render homage to religion, and to have chanters of their exploits, the kings and chiefs of the tribes recalled the bards from the heart of the forests. The function of the druids, of an inferior rank, was to sing the gods and heroes. The conquerors, jealous of immortalizing their names, spared these dispensers of glory; attracted them into their camps; where gratitude and rewards animated the bards to paint their protectors as heroes endowed with all virtues. Those druids were admitted to a knowledge of science, and associated in the mysteries of the first pontiffs. Their genius and knowledge elevated them above the vulgar. They consecrated their songs to the picture of all virtues and all heroic sentiments. The kings were eager to take for their models the heroes of the poems imagined by the bards. The chiefs of tribes strove to equal the kings; and this noble emulation, communicating itself to the whole nation, formed the general characteristic of the inhabitants of Great Britain, who, at all times have known how to unite lofty valour with the finest virtues of civilized nations.

The glory of a great nation awakens the genius of the man whom nature has endowed with a glowing imagination; and he burns with the idea of immortalizing his country. Vulgar language appears to him to fall below the dignity of those actions which he wishes to celebrate. He knows that measure and harmony will more easily impress his sentiments on the memory: and hence, no doubt, is the origin of poetry among all nations; an art which constituted a considerable portion of the religion of the Druids.

The practice among all nations, of repeating historic poems on solemn occasions, and of causing children to learn them, has been the mean of preserving them long without the help of writing.

The ancient Germans transmitted, until the eighth century, poetical traditions by this means.

It is not, then, to be wondered at, that the inhabitants of Great Britain, always so attached to the remembrance of their ancestors, should have transmitted from generation to generation, the poems of their bards. It is to that usage, continued among the remote inhabitants of the mountains, that Macpherson owed the possibility of collecting the poesies of the celebrated Ossian.

After having long been the first instructers and the early historians of their country, the bards descended from those high offices to that of being the flatterers of those who protected them, or the slanderers of those whom they looked upon as their enemies.

Petty passions have always the fatal tendency of misleading, and frequently of even extinguishing, genius. The bards, forgetting the noble inspirations of their predecessors, sought no other employment than that of amusing and flattering self-love: and even pride itself grows weary of the praises of which it inwardly acknowledges itself unworthy. The great soon learned to despise the mean flatteries of the bards. They were welcomed only by the multitude; but not having talents enough to paint truth in interesting colours, they had recourse to puerile inventions. The wonderful ridicule of bewitching castles, fairies, and giants, succeeded the sublimest conceptions of real poetry, until their folly and trash disgusted even the common people themselves. Hence, they forsook the bards, who nearly disappeared.

The warriors, nevertheless, preserved their valour, and would not altogether renounce the brilliant honour of hearing their exploits celebrated. Courage, and the noble desire of assisting the oppressed and of redressing grievances, caused the spirit of chivalry to spring up. It produced prodigies of heroism, and great actions revived the genius of some. These came to replace the bards, under the name of Troubadours. And, this appears to be a suitable place to drop a remark on the origin of those romances of chivalry, so singular and so extravagantly beautiful, that they still raise our admiration. In reading them, we are almost at a stand concerning their truth. What an idea must we have of knights, who wished to be painted in the *romances of the Round Table, of the St. Greal, of the Amadis*, and so on!

It is worthy of remark, that it was in Great Britain, that the Troubadours and the old romancers, the heroes of the early romances of chivalry, first arose. It may also be observed, that al the historians, after having represented the druids as pontiffs, far superior to others, unite in placing the druids of England above the druids of other countries. They extol those of the college of Chartres, those of the forest of Marseilles, and of the environs of Toulouse; but assert that, when in those colleges, there was proposed a subject which involved deep discussion, it was sent to be examined in the school of the druids of Great Britain. From this series of observations, it appears that, from the most ancient times, the inhabitants of Great Britain have astonished the rest of the world by their wisdom, their knowledge, and their bravery.

RELIGIOUS TENETS OF THE PRIMITIVE INHABITANTS OF GREAT BRITAIN.

It appears evident that the early Britons raised no temples to divinity. It is even found in the poesies of Ossian that this sublime bard shows contempt for the temples and worship of Odin, god of the Scandinavians, whom he calls Loda. Ossian represents those people as invoking their god, around a statue which he calls the *"stone of power"*. He condemns this worship, and considers it as impious. The Druids, the bards, and the people whom they instructed, considered all nature as the temple of divinity. It cannot be doubted that they had ideas of the existence of a Supreme Being, since they believed in the immortality of the soul, and in the rewards and punishments of another life.

According to their notions, the clouds were the

residence of souls after their separation from the body. Valiant and virtuous men were received with joy into *the ethereal palaces of their fathers*, while the wicked, the slothful, and the barbarous, were excluded from the residence of the heroes, and condemned to wander over the winds. There were different apartments in the palaces of the clouds. Merit and bravery obtained the first; and this idea tended to redouble the emulation of warriors. The soul preserved the same tastes as during life. In the ethereal state of existence, though in a higher degree, were conferred the same honours as on earth.

It was thought that departed souls commanded the winds and tempests; but that their power was not extended over men. A hero could never enter into the palace of his fathers, unless he had sung over him the funeral hymn. This hymn appears to have been the only essential ceremony of their obsequies. The body was laid on a bed of clay, in the bottom of a ditch six or eight feet deep. By the side of a warrior were placed his sword and twelve arrows. His body was again covered with a second bed of clay, upon which a wooden stag, or some other wild beast, was placed. Sometimes his favorite mastiff was killed to be placed on the claybed, and covered with a piece of select earth, and four stones ranged on the four sides, which marked the extent of the tomb.

A bard alone could open the gates of the ethereal palace, by singing the funeral hymn. The neglect of this ceremony, left the soul in the mists of the lake Lego, or of some other water, and to the forgotten and unfortunate souls were attributed the frequent and sometimes mortal diseases which are caused by the vapours of lakes and marshes. People foresaw with what care the bards kept up the opinions which rendered their ministry so consolatory and so necessary.

It was not thought that death could break the bonds of blood and friendship. The shades were interested in all the fortunate or unfortunate events of their living friends. No nation has given stronger belief in apparitions. The mountaineers, above all, delighted with the most gloomy ideas, and often went to spend nights upon the heaths; where the whistling of the winds and the noise of the torrents caused them to imagine that they heard the voices of the dead; and when sleep came to surprise them amidst their reveries, they considered their dreams as certain presages of futurity.

The good and evil spirits did not appear in the same manner: the good showed themselves to their friends during the daytime, and in smiling and solitary vales; the evil, never appeared but in the night, amidst storms and winds.

Death did not destroy the charms of the beautiful. Their shades preserved the traits and forms of their earthly beauty: terror never surrounded them; and, when they traversed the air, their motions were graceful, and the light noise which was heard, was gentle and soothing. At the moment of executing any great undertaking, the souls of fathers were thought to descend from their clouds, and come to predict good or ill success: and although they did not suffer themselves to be perceived, yet they gave warnings by some kind of omen. Every man believed he had his tutelary shade that incessantly followed him. When death was approaching him, the protecting spirit appeared to him in the situation where he was to die, and uttered plaintive cries. At the death of great personages, it was believed that the souls of departed bards sung for three nights about his phantom.

It was generally thought that, as soon as a warrior ceased to exist, the arms which he had at home, appeared to be stained with blood; that his shade visited the place of his birth, and appeared to his mastiff, which made doleful howlings at its aspect.

The most natural effects which their ignorance could not comprehend were attributed to the agency of spirits. The echo which struck upon the ear was the voice of the spirit of the mountain. The deafening noise which precedes tempests was the roaring of the spirit of the hill. If the wind made the harps of bards resound, it was the shades, who, by that light touch, predicted the death of a great personage. A chief or a king never lost his life, unless the harps of the bards attached to his family, rendered that prophetic sound. How pleasant it must have appeared to one, to believe all nature peopled with the shades of his ancestors and friends, and to fancy himself constantly surrounded by them. In spite of all the melancholy which such ideas inspired, yet how deeply interesting and touchingly charming they must have been! They were enough to feast and fill up the most poetic imagination. It is to that cause that we must, no doubt, attribute the smallness of the number of deities which were honoured in England. It appears very evident, that Esus, Dis, Pluto, Samothes, Teutates, and various other gods, had not come to their knowledge until by their communication with foreigners. The Picts and the Saxons acquainted them with their Andate, the goddes of victory: the Romans also brought them some of their gods. Tacitus and Dion Cassius assure us, that it was the Gauls who brought into England the horrible custom of immolating human victims. In farther extending our researches, we might also find among them vestiges of the worship of the Phœnicians; for we have ample proof, that in very remote times, those first navigators of the world, brought their goods into Great Britain, and exchanged them for lead and tin. But we need not enter on farther particulars in relation to the worship they acquired from foreigners, since all historians, all their traditions, and all their customs, sufficiently prove that the religion of the Druids, was the only one that was generally adopted.

We will now occupy the reader for a few moments by presenting what history and tradition have preserved and transmitted as certain, with respect to that class of men so singular and celebrated — the Druids.

OF THE DRUIDS.

Cesar and Tacitus contradict each other; the former, by saying that the religion of the Druids had its birth in England; the latter, by alleging that the Gauls in peopling that island carried their mysteries with them.

In order to reconcile the two authors, says the Abbé Banier, it may be supposed that the Gauls in passing into England, carried thither their religion; but that those islanders, being more reflecting, and less warlike, than the Gauls, preserved it in its purity. Such, adds he, is the origin of the profound respect which the Druids of Gaul had for those of England, whom they considered as their superiors.

The world, continues the Abbé, at first formed but one common family, and had but one creed. In separating from each other, men changed their primitive religion, and lost its purity. Some, coming by land from the North, under the name of Scythians, Celtic-Scythians, and Celts, peopled the vast regions which separate us from Asia; others, more bold, attempted the perils of the sea. History informs us that the Phœnicians and Carthaginians penetrated even into the heart of the west: and hence, no doubt, that resemblance of worship among people so widely separated, both by sea and land.

This view clearly explains the parallel which has often been drawn between the Magi and the Druids, and shows that the Gauls might have held the religion of the Persians, or, at least, of the people who bordered on them by the North.

The Magi and the Druids, equally venerated in their respective countries, were always consulted on matters of great importance. They were equally the sole ministers of their religion. The Magi rejected the opinion which gives to the gods a human origin, and did not separate them into gods and goddesses. It was the same with the Druids. Both governed the state, and the kings consulted them. Their white garbs were alike. Golden ornaments were equally interdicted to them. As the organs and distributors of justice, they passed sentences, and watched over those whom they loaded with that august function. .

The immortality of the soul was the capital point of belief among both the Persians and the Gauls: both had neither temples nor statues. The Persians adored the fire; the Druids kept up a perpetual fire in their forests. The Persians rendered to the water a religious worship; and the Gauls likewise rendered the same honours to that element. These resemblances are sufficient to make it appear evident that the religion of the Magi and that of the Druids had the same origin; the differences between them might have been easily caused by wars, separation, and time.

The religion of the Gauls appears to have always been purer than that of other heathen nations.' Their ideas on divinity were much more, just and spiritual than those of the Greeks and Romans. Tacitus, Maximus Tyrius, and other historians, inform us that the Druids believed the Supreme Being ought to be honoured by respect and silence, as well as by sacrifices; but that primitive simplicity continued only until the conquests of the Romans. The Druids, forgetting their primitive wisdom, became addicted to divination and magic, and tolerated those horrible sacrifices in which human victims were immolated to Esus and Teutates. Tacitus, Lactantius, and Lucian, attest to this cruel degradation.

The conquests of Julius Cesar introduced new gods into Gaul; and the first temples were at that time built there, whilst the British Druids continued the exercise of their antique religion, amidst the forests, the majestic shades of which inspired religious awe and holy fear. Those woods were so sacred among them, that it was not permitted to cut them down. No one could approach them but with a religious respect, though for the purpose of adorning them with flowers and trophies. People could not employ for ordinary purposes, certain trees, even when they fell with old age. That respect clung to the grand idea that they had divinity; and they were persuaded that temples could not include it, nor statues represent it.

The Gauls had the highest respect for lakes and marshes, because they thought that divinity loved to inhabit them. The most celebrated of those lakes, was that of Toulouse, into which they cast gold and silver, taken from their enemies. To this worship was joined that of rivers, creeks, fountains, and fire.

In the middle of those forests, the Gauls had spaces consecrated to worship and to religious ceremonies. It was there that they buried treasures taken from their enemies; and also, that prisoners were immolated, enclosed in colossuses of osier, and afterwards surrounded with combustible materials, and consumed by fire. Cesar caused those secret places to be plundered by his troops. Hence, misinformed historians have asserted, that the ancient Gauls had temples. ""Those people," says " Tacitus ", "have nothing for their temple but a forest, where they discharge the duties of their religion. No one can enter into that wood, unless he bears a chain, a mark of his dependence, and of the supreme dominion which God has over him.""

Nothing is more celebrated in the history of the ancient Gauls than the forests of the country of Chartres. The forests of Marseilles and Toulouse were almost as noted. In the middle of them were held the schools of the Druids of Gaul. Chartres was, as it were, the metropolis of Gaul; but those three colleges united in acknowledging the superiority of the knowledge which the Druids of Great Britain had over them.

OF THE DIFFERENT CLASSES OF PRIESTS; THEIR MANNER OF LIVING; THEIR DRESS AND FUNCTIONS.

The name Druids comes, no doubt, from the Celtic word *deru*, which means *oak*. The religious instructers of the ancient Britons were, divided into different classes. The Druids composed the first class. They were the supreme chiefs; so that the inferior orders were entirely subject to their will, and could not even remain in their presence, unless they had obtained their permission. The inferior ministers were the *Bards*, the *Saronides*, and the *Cubages* or *Vates*.

The Bards, whose Celtic name means a *chanter*, celebrated in verse the actions of heroes, and sung them accompanied by the harp. So great value was attached to their verses, that they were often the means of immortalizing them. The Bards, though less powerful than the Druids, enjoyed so high consideration, that if they presented themselves at the moment in which two armies were going to combat, or even after they had commenced it, they laid down their arms to listen to their advice. The Bards were not wholly confined to sing the praises of heroes; but they had likewise the right of censuring the actions of those who swerved from the path of duty.

The Saronides instructed youth, and inspired them with virtuous sentiments.

The Cubages or Vates had the care of sacrifices, and applied themselves to the contemplation of nature. In time, the Druids reserved for themselves alone the offices of religion, and the subaltern ministers exercised no other functions than those granted by the Druids.

The origin of those pontiffs is lost in the remotest antiquity. Aristotle, Phocion, and many others before them, describe them as men among the wisest and most enlightened in matters of religion. So high an idea was entertained of their learning, that Cicero considers them the inventors of mythology.

The Druids, hidden in their forests, led an austere life. Thither the nations went to consult them; and Julius Cesar, who usually admired nothing but what was splendid, was so astonished at their manner of living and their science, that he could not withhold from them his esteem.

The Druids formed different colleges in Gaul; the most celebrated of which was that of the country of Chartres, whose chief was the sovereign pontiff of Gaul. It was in the forests of that country that the greatest sacrifices were offered up, and the great men and generals of the country assembled. Both young and old among the Druids, conformed to the same principles and the same rules. Their clothing differed a little according to the provinces in which they lived, and the degrees which they held.

The ceremony of entering upon the profession, was performed by their receiving the embrace of the old Druids. The candidate, after having passed through it, exchanged his usual dress for that of the Druids, which was a tunic falling half way down the legs. This dress designated priesthood, to which women could never be admitted.

The authority of the Druids was so great, that none undertook any important affair without consulting them. They presided over the state; decided upon peace and war at pleasure; punished the guilty; and could depose magistrates and even kings, when they did not observe the laws of the country. Their rank was superior to that of nobles. All bowed before them; and it was to their care that the education of the most distinguished youths was entrusted; so that they prepared them, from early life, to be impressed with a deep sense of respect for the Druids.

To them belonged the right of appointing those who were to govern cities. They could raise one of those magistrates even to the dignity of vergobret, which equalled that of a king; but this pretended king could do nothing without the advice of the Druids. They alone convoked the council; so that the vergobrets were merely the ministers and the first subjects of the Druids.

The supreme arbiters of all differences, and all the interests of the people, justice was administered only by their ministry. They decided equally on public and private affairs. When, in a law-suit, they adjudged a disputed estate to him whom they designated as the legitimate possessor, his adversary was obliged to submit, or he was struck with an anathema, and then all sacrifice was interdicted to him; the whole nation considered him as impious, and dared no longer to communicate with him.

As the Druids were charged with all the high offices of religion, their power was unbounded. Sacrifices, offerings, public and private prayers, the science of predicting future events, the care of consulting the gods, of replying in their names, and of studying nature; the right of establishing new ceremonies and new laws, of watching over the execution of the old, or of reforming them, were the offices and the unlimited powers which they enjoyed undisputed.

Their state dispensed with their going to war, and exempted them from all taxes. The number of aspirants after that order was immense, and all classes and professions were admitted; but they were checked by the great length of probation demanded, and by the indispensable necessity of learning and retaining in memory the prodigious number of verses which contained their maxims on religion and political economy.

Anciently, Gallic women could be admitted to the rank of Druidesses, and enjoy all the prerogatives of the order; but they exercised their functions separately from men. Their divination had, at one time, rendered them more celebrated than the Druids themselves.

When Hannibal passed into Gaul, they still enjoyed supreme rights; for it was said in a treaty which he made with the Gauls: ""If a Carthaginian should do wrong to a Gaul, the cause would be brought to the tribunal of Gallic women."" In aftertimes, the Druids stripped them of that authority; but the epoch of this usurpation is unknown.

DOCTRINE OF THE DRUIDS; THEIR SUPERSTITIONS; CEREMONY OF THE OAK-MISLETOE.

The doctrines of the Druids tended to render men wise, just, valiant, and religious. The fundamental points were reduced to three: Worship the gods; Injure no body; and Be courageous. Their sciences, says Pomponius Mela, was to know the form and greatness of the Supreme Being, the course of the stars and of their revolutions. They pretended to know the whole of the universe; and the retirement in which they lived, allowed them all the time necessary to inform themselves.

It cannot be doubted that the Druids and the Gauls generally, considered the soul as immortal; and it was the belief in that sublime truth, which caused them to consider death as a sure means of attaining to a more happy life. They made a great difference between those who died peaceably amidst their relatives and friends, and those who lost their life in serving their country. The former were interred without ceremony, without eulogy, without songs of honour. It was thought that when warriors lost their lives, and that their names were transmitted to future generations, they departed to taste an eternal happiness in the bosom of divinity. They had tombs and epitaphs. But the blessings of the immortality of the soul were not to be universal. They, who had adorned their lives by no exploit, either warlike or splendid, or otherwise contributing to the general good, were considered as condemned to oblivion. This illiberal idea sprung out of the warlike genius of the Gauls and other Celts, who followed nothing but the profession of arms.

The Druids taught that one day water and fire would destroy all things. They believed in the doctrine of metempsychosis, which they could not have learned from Pythagoras, since they taught it long before that philosopher travelled into Gaul.

From time immemorial, they were accustomed to bury the dead, or to enclose their ashes in urns. They placed in the tombs, the arms of the dead, their valuable furniture, and the cedula of money which they had lent. They wrote even letters to their friends, though dead. One of their superstitions was that every letter cast into the tomb, arrived as directed.

The Druids orally communicated their sciences and their doctrines to their candidates, whose novitiate was extremely long. They never wrote down their maxims, nor any thing appertaining to their sciences. They arranged and digested all sorts of knowledge inverse; and those verses were to be committed to memory. These were so numerous, that frequently fifteen and even twenty years were passed in learning and retaining them. The doctrine of the Druids, says Julius Cæsar, was mysterious, and could be known to nobody.

The Druids also cultivated the science of medicine. Upon, this point, the people yielded them unlimited confidence, because they were persuaded that they knew the influence of the stars, and could see into futurity. Those sages, so highly respected at first, and so worthy of respect, ended with being addicted to astrology, magic, and divination, in the hope of thereby increasing their credit and authority. They maintained that people are always more fond of the marvellous than of truth. They had some knowledge of botany; but they mingled so many superstitious practices with the manner in which they collected their plants, as left it easy to be perceived, that they were acquainted with only a very small number of them. Pliny relates the manner in which they collected the *selage*: it must be plucked without a knife, and with the right hand, which must be covered with a part of the robe; and then made to pass into the left with swiftness, as if it had been stolen. The one who gathered it, must, moreover, be barefoot, and dressed in white, having previously offered a sacrifice of bread and wine.

The vervain was collected before sunrise on the first day of the dog-star, after one had offered to Earth a sacrifice of expiation in which they employed fruits and honey. This plant having been thus collected, possessed, they believed, every virtue, and healed all diseases; and if one rubbed himself with it, he could obtain all he wished. It had power to conciliate hearts alienated by enmity; and all whom that plant touched, instantly felt peace and gaiety spring up in their breast.

It is also necessary to range among the number of their superstitions, their persuasion that, at the death of great personages, their souls excited storms and tempests. The noise of thunder, all the extraordinary and violent motions of nature, all meteors, announced, according to them, the death of a great personage.

The Druids delighted in making it believed that they could change into any form at will, and cause themselves to be transported through the air; but the most cruel of all their superstitions, was that of immolating human victims. This barbarous usage could not be abolished but by the extinction of druidism. The numerous edicts of the Roman emperors against this crime, not only prove its existence, but also show how pertinaciously they persisted in it.

The most solemn of all their ceremonies, was that of collecting the oak-misletoe. This parasite plant grows on several other trees; but the Druids thought that God had chiefly chosen the oak to entrust to it that valuable plant. They ran over the forests and looked for it with the greatest care; and felicitated themselves when, after long and painful searches, they discovered a certain quantity of it.

They could not collect that plant except in the month of December, and on the sixth day of the moon. This month and the number six were sacred among them. It was always on the sixth of the moon that they made their principal acts of devotion.

On the day intended for the ceremony of collecting the misletoe, they assembled with great rejoicing, and went in procession towards the places where the plant was found, two diviners marching forward singing hymns and canticles. A herald, carrying a caduceus, came after them. Three Druids followed him, and carried instruments necessary for sacrifice; and, in fine the chief of the pontiffs, clothed in a white robe, with an immense crowd marching in his train, closed the procession. When they were arrived at the foot of the tree, the chief of the Druids mounted on the oak, cut the misletoe with a golden sickle, and the other Druids received it with great respect into the *sagum*, a kind of white coat of mail.

After having received it, they immolated two white bulls. A festival ensued; and when it was over, they addressed prayers to divinity that it would infuse into that plant a happiness which might be felt by those to whom particles of it should be distributed.

This misletoe was consecrated and distributed to the people on the first day of the year.

PRINCIPAL MAXIMS OF THE DRUIDS.

In giving the principal maxims of the Druids, it must be observed, that we present them as they have come down to us by tradition, since the Druids never wrote them. It is even probable that they were composed after the time stated by ancient authority.

1. Their maxims must be taught in thick groves by sacred priests.

2. The misletoe ought to be collected with great ceremony, and always, if possible, on the sixth day of the moon, and a golden sickle must be made use of to cut it;

3. All that are born derive their origin from heaven.

4. The secret of the sciences must not be entrusted to writing, but merely to memory

5. The education of children must be carefully attended to.

6. The disobedient ought to be removed from sacrifices.

7. Souls are immortal.

8. Souls pass into other bodies after the death of those which they have animated.

9. If the world perish, it will be by water or by fire.

10. On extraordinary occasions a man must be immolated. One can read futurity according as the body falls, as the blood flows, or as the wound is opened.

11. Prisoners of war should be immolated on altars, or enclosed in osier baskets to be burned alive in honour of the gods.

12. Intercourse with foreigners must not be permitted.

13. He who arrives last in the assembly of the states is to be punished with death.

14. Children should be raised up until the age of fourteen out of the presence of their parents.

15. Money lent in this life, will be rendered to creditors in the other world.

16. There is another world, and those who kill themselves to accompany their friends, will live there with them.

17. All letters given at the dying hour, or cast

into funeral piles, are faithfully returned to the world.

18. Let the disobedient be driven away; let them recive no justice; let them be received into no employment.

19. All fathers of families are kings in their houses; and have the power of life and death over their wives, children, and slaves.

Such are the principal maxims collected and inculcated by the Druids. A glance at them is sufficient to enable us to perceive how easy it was for those pontiffs to command opinion, and subjugate the mind — them who controlled the education of youth, and hurled their anathemas against all who dared to disobey or oppose them.

OF THE DRUIDESSES.

We have already said that the whole system of the morality of the Druids was reduced to three principal points: Honour to the gods, injury to no one, and courage. But it is not easy to reconcile with these sublime maxims, that which gave to fathers the right of life and death over their wives, their children, and slaves. Paternal and domestic authority, says the Abbé Banier, is founded upon no positive law, but only in love and respect. Julius Cesar and Tacitus delight in eulogizing the respect which the Gauls and Germans had for their wives; but the wives of the Druids sometimes shared the authority of their husbands. They were often consulted in political and religious affairs. There were in Gaul temples erected, even since the conquests of the Romans, in which the Druidesses alone ordained and regulated all that related to religion, and whose entrance was interdicted to the men.

The Celts and Gauls, says Mr. Mallet in his excellent *Introduction to the History of Denmark,* have shown themselves, in their treatment of the softer sex, far superior to the orientals, who pass from adoration to contempt, and from the sentiments of an idolatrous love to those of an inhuman jealousy, or to those of an indifference more insulting than jealousy. The Celts considered their women as equals, and companions whose esteem and tenderness could not be acquired but by tender regard and generous treatment.

The poesies of Ossian show that the ancient inhabitants of the British isles, carried that respect and those virtuous regards as far as any other nation. Faithful to the one which their heart had chosen, they never had several wives at once: and often the wife in disguise followed her hero to war.

In the brilliant times of chivalry, we find that the same views of those morals, and of that same respect for women, still existed: and gratitude often followed in the train of such noble sentiments; for as soon as a knight was wounded, ladies were eager to serve him; and almost all understood the art of dressing wounds. But they were not confined to those kind offices. During the time of convalescence, the charm of their conversation served to inflame the courage of the knights; and in order to recall heroic enterprizes to their remembrance, they read to them poems and romances, into which was infused all the fire and ardour that heroism could produce.

We have no doubt of the existence of that atrocious maxim which gave the Druids the horrible right of employing force to oppress and sometimes slaughter helpless innocence. Those pontiffs were jealous of their authority, although it was so great and so well established, that, to maintain it, they did not need to be cruel in their families. All the people fell at their feet, and no human being was above their power. How, then, could they delight in filling with terror their female companions, who alone could give charms to their solitude; or those children that were to perpetuate their memory; or their slaves, who watched to anticipate and satisfy all their wants? This cruel maxim, therefore, if it did exist among the Druids and the Gauls, could not have belonged to them, but at the time of their greatest degradation.

There existed three kinds of Druidesses: the first lived in celibacy; the second, though married, remained in temples, where they cleared tables, and did not see their husbands but for one day in the year; the third did not quit their husbands, and took care of the domestic affairs of the temple.

But notwithstanding these distinctions, the Druidesses really formed but two classes. The first was composed of priestesses; and the second were the attendants of the priestesses, whose orders they were to execute.

The most ordinary residence of the Druidesses was in the isles which bordered on the coasts of Gaul and England. The Druids also inhabited them; and there the Druids and Druidesses exercised themselves most in magic. The people of Gaul and England generally believed that they could raise storms and tempests at pleasure.

The restless curiosity of men places the power of reading in the hook of fate, above any other. The Druids, after having persuaded the people that they understood the influence of the stars, and could read future events, abandoned almost entirely to their wives this portion of their ministry.

The almost idolatrous veneration which the Gauls and Germans had for their women, caused them to imagine, that they possessed more highly than themselves, the gift of persuading and making their predictions believed in. Accordingly, they sent them all questions on futurity; to which they returned so judicious answers, that their reputation was spread over the whole world. People came from every quarter to consult them; and their decisions inspired infinitely more confidence than the oracles of Greece and Italy. The emperors, after they became masters of Gaul, often caused them to be consulted. History has preserved a great number of their replies; but it makes no particular mention of those of the Druids.

We shall close this article by citing what is well known respecting the period in which the order of the Druids and Druidesses became wholly abolished.

Suetonius, Aurelius Victor, and Seneca, maintain, that it was in the reign of Claudius; but, as they actually existed, much longer, it appears that these authors intended to speak only of the abolition of human sacrifices, the use of which that emperor interdicted. The Druids were found in the country of Chartrain until the middle of the fifth century. It appears that their order became extinct, not until the time in which Christianity completely triumphed over the superstitions of the Gauls; and this triumph took place in some provinces, but at a very late period.

Copyright © 2021 by FV Editions
Book Cover : *Tor's Fight
with the Giants*, Mårten Eskil Winge.
Drawing before 1st chapter : *Odin and his two brothers create the
world out of the body of Ymir*, Lorenz Frølich
Ebook ISBN: 979-10-299-1323-5
Paperback ISBN: 979-10-299-1324-2
All rights reserved.

www.ingramcontent.com/pod-product-compliance
Lightning Source LLC
LaVergne TN
LVHW031607060526
838201LV00063B/4757